SERMON OUTLINES ON THE NAMES & CHARACTER OF GOD

Charles R. Wood

KREGEL PUBLICATIONS

Grand Rapids, Michigan 49501

Sermon Outlines on the Names and Character of God, by Charles R. Wood. © 1991 by Kregel Publications, a division of Kregel, Inc., P. O. Box 2607, Grand Rapids, MI 49501. All rights reserved.

Cover: Don Ellens

Library of Congress Cataloging-in-Publication Data

Wood, Charles R. (Charles Robert), 1933–
Sermon outlines on the names and character of God / Charles R. Wood.
    p.   cm.—(Easy-to-use sermon outline series)
  Includes index.
  1. God—Name—Sermons—Outlines, syllabi, etc.
2. God—Attributes—Sermons—Outlines, syllabi, etc.
I. Title. II. Series: Wood, Charles R. (Charles Robert),
1933-   Easy-to-use sermon outline series.

BT180.N2W66   1991   231'.4—dc20   91-27156
                                                        CIP
ISBN   0-8254-3990-6 (pbk.)

      1 2 3 4 5 Printing/Year 95 94 93 92 91

Printed in the United States of America

Introduction

Jonathan Edwards's famous sermon, "Sinners in the Hands of an Angry God," spoke with thundering conviction to his day and resulted in many significant decisions. Unfortunately, that sermon would likely have little or no effect were it to be preached today. There is little awareness of God and even less interest in Him in our day, and there is virtually no belief in God's intervention in the affairs of men or in the means that He might use in that intervention. In brief, God has fallen on hard times in the thinking of modern man. Someone has said that Edwards, preaching today, might be forced to title his sermon, "God in the Hands of Angry Sinners."

Although it would not generally be admitted, God has not fared much better in the church than He has in the world. Theology is no longer the "queen of the sciences," having been relegated to a place among many "necessary" studies and assigned an importance somewhat below that accorded to pastoral studies, musicology and even courses in management practice. It has been assigned such modifiers as "Process," "Liberation," and "Dynamic," and the modification has been more than that of a mere part of speech.

A national religion of secular humanism leaves little room for God in society in general, and its pernicious influences subtly invade the hearts of God's people, leaving small place for Him among His own. How great is the need in our day for a return to a biblical understanding of God! The simple truth is that all the attempts to eliminate, dilute, rationalize, debunk, and ignore God have had absolutely no effect on the fact that God exists and that He continues to operate in His relationships to man and his world in exactly the same ways recorded for us in the Bible.

The sermons in this book are an attempt to discern biblical teaching regarding God and to make application of that teaching in ways relevant to modern man. There is no desire or effort to bring God down to man's level; the exact opposite is actually the case. It is the conviction of the editor that the time has come to stress the exaltation of God and to put the burden of knowing God on the men to whom He has already revealed Himself.

The book begins with a series of sermons on the names of God. That series is not totally exhaustive as a few of the lesser-known names of God do not readily lend themselves to preaching. The series on the names of God is followed by a group of messages which deal with the character of God and the ways in which He relates to mankind in general and to His people in particular.

All the sermons in this book are the work of its author (although I am obviously indebted to the commentators, etc., whose work I constantly consult to determine the accuracy of interpretations and applications). They are sermons which have been preached from the pulpit of Grace Baptist Church in South Bend, Indiana, so they are "tried" in the truest sense of the word. They are not designed to be preached "as is." The best results will be derived from a careful study of the passages on which they are based, using the outlines as an aid in organizing the presentation of the material studied.

In a day of great indifference concerning the God of the universe, these messages are offered as a token of praise to God and with the hope that they may contribute at least minutely to a renewed emphasis on the person and work of God that might in turn reshape the face of the church and retool its impact on a needy world.

Contents

The Names of God: Elohim—Genesis 1 7

The Names of God: El Shaddai—Genesis 17:1-8 9

The Names of God: Jehovah—Exodus 3:13 &14 10

The Names of God: Jehovah-M'Kaddesh—Leviticus 20:8 11

The Names of God: Adonai—Deuteronomy 10:17-20 13

The Names of God: Jehovah-Rophe—Exodus 15:22-26 14

The Names of God: Jehovah-Shalom—Judges 6:24 16

The Names of God: Jehovah-Rohi—Psalm 23 18

The Names of God: Jehovah-Tsidkenu—Jeremiah 23:1-6 19

The Names of God: Jehovah-Shammah—Ezekiel 48:35 21

The Provision of God—Genesis 6:8-22 22

God's Dealings—Genesis 7 24

The Goodness of God—Genesis 8 26

God Who Demands Obedience—Genesis 11:26-12:5 28

God The Rewarder of Right—Genesis 13:5-18 30

Knowing God—Genesis 15:1-21 32

God's Self-Revelation—Genesis 18 34

God Is—Genesis 23 & 24 36

God's Tests—Genesis 26:1-5 38

The Self-Existence of God—Exodus 3:1-4 40

The God of The Burning Bush—Exodus 3:1-5 42

God's Assurances—Exodus 5:22-6:30 43

The Sovereignty of God—Exodus 14 45

Let God Be God—Exodus 19:9-25 47

The Dark Side of God?—Exodus 20:5 & 6 49

HIs Name in Vain—Exodus 20:7 51

Utterly Awesome—Deuteronomy 4:9-14 52

No Similitude—Deuteronomy 4:15-28 54

Divine Rights—Psalm 24:1-6 56

The Perfection of God—Psalm 138:8 58

Like a Shepherd—Isaiah 40:11 59

Our Incomparable God—Isaiah 40:18, 25; 46:5 61
The Jealousy of God—Ezekiel 39:25 63

Textual Index

Genesis 1:26 7
Genesis 2 10
Genesis 2:4 7
Genesis 3:16 26
Genesis 9:1-8 26
Genesis 9:5, 6 26
Genesis 9:12-17 26
Genesis 15:1, 2 13
Genesis 43:3, 4 38
Exodus 3 10
Exodus 4:10 13
Exodus 10:5 63
Exodus 12:43-45 13
Exodus 19:9-13, 16, 18-20 52
Exodus 19:21-24 52
Exodus 20:3-5a 54
Exodus 20:18-20 52
Exodus 32:13 13
Exodus 34:7 49
Exodus 34:14 63
Leviticus 1—7 10
Leviticus 20:23 11
Leviticus 20:24 11
Leviticus 20:25 11
Leviticus 20:26 11
Numbers 14:18 49
Deuteronomy 4:24 63
Deuteronomy 5:9 ....49, 63
Deuteronomy 6:4 7
Deuteronomy 6:15 63
Deuteronomy 10:18, 19 13
Deuteronomy 10:20b 13

Deuteronomy 24:16 49
Joshua 1:9 21
Joshua 24:19 63
1 Samuel 19
1 Samuel 17:34-36 60
Psalm 36:1 52
Psalm 115:8 55
Psalm 123:2 13
Isaiah 6:1-8 13
Isaiah 6:8 7
Isaiah 40:12 61
Isaiah 40:13, 14 61
Jeremiah 21 19
Ezekiel 18:20 49
Malachi 1:6 13
Mark 6:34 60
Luke 12:4, 5 53
John 7:17 47
John 10:11 60
John 10:11-14 59
John 13:13-16 13
Acts 9:6 13
1 Corinthians 10:13 22
2 Corinthians 5:11 52
2 Corinthians 7:1 52
Ephesians 5:21 52
Hebrews 11:13 36
Hebrews 12:28 52
Hebrews 13:20 59
1 Peter 1:17 52
1 Peter 2:17 52
1 Peter 5:4 59

The Names of God: Elohim

Genesis 1

Introduction:
What's in a name? A name identifies a person. A name also limits a person. This is why God has so many different names in Scripture. The first name used in the Bible is Elohim, and it is used more than 2,250 times. There is much in that name.

I. **Plurality**
   A. It is often said that the Trinity is a New Testament doctrine
      1. The Jews do not hold it at all
      2. The Liberals reject it
   B. Elohim is a strange noun
      1. Genesis 1:26 has plural form
      2. It is often used with a singular: Isaiah 6:8
      3. Singularity clearly expressed in Deuteronomy 6:4
   C. The simple truth: God is one entity who exists in three persons. This is difficult to explain and impossible to understand

II. **Power**
   A. It likely comes from El
      1. A word of great power
      2. A word that stresses God above all
   B. Elohim is used in conjunction with creation
      1. It is used thirty-five times before Genesis 2:4
      2. It is the name for God used in the section
   C. It explains the first commandment
      1. The created is always less than the Creator
      2. A graven image detracts from the Creator who is great above all greatness

III. **Personalized**
   A. There is an element of "Alyah" in the word as well
      1. It comes from "covenant"
      2. A covenant is an agreement between two people with God as witness or between God and a person
   B. God exists in covenant with mankind
      1. He provides most of the agreement
      2. Little is required of us
         a. Faithful trust
         b. Obedience: "no knowledge in the world is commendable but as it is digested into will and reduced into practice"
   C. Incredible covenant

1. I am in personal relationship with a God so great I cannot even comprehend Him adequately
2. I am in covenant with the triune God and all the benefits of all His persons are mine

Conclusion:

Elohim speaks of God Almighty. Elohim speaks of Almighty-God in covenant relationship with His children. Through faith in Christ I have become personally related to the Almighty God. Surely my Christianity has to mean more to me than a casual "tip of the hat" once a week.

The Names of God: El Shaddai

Genesis 17:1-8

Introduction:

What's in a name? A name identifies. A name reveals (especially a biblical name). A name limits. Because God is so big, many names are necessary. Look at El-Shaddai.

I. **What It Does Not Mean**
   A. The translation does not adequately cover it
   B. Almightiness is already covered by El
   C. We need to discern the meaning of Shaddai

II. **What It Does Mean**
   A. Shaddai—word for female breast
   B. "Almighty God of the breast"
   C. It has reference to some functions of God:
      1. He is the bestower of life
      2. He is the provider of sustenance
      3. He is the donator of fruitfulness
      4. Simply stated it points up the "blessing" aspect of God
   D. Clarification
      1. The story of Abraham in passage
      2. All else is now dead and gone; now God will show Himself as the giver of life

III. **What It All Means**
   A. It draws attention to the source of all blessings
      1. Every blessing comes from God
      2. God is our absolute final source for anything and everything
   B. It focuses on the character of God
      1. God's primary desire is to bless
      2. Everything that comes from God and is allowed by God is designed for good
   C. It emphasizes God's ability
      1. God can do anything we need done
      2. God can and will back up His promises because He must
   D. It stresses a warning: blessings can become a curse when not properly received

Conclusion:

Whatever it is you need, God can provide it. God is the only source of blessings. God's blessings are all we need. How are you relating to the blessing of God?

9

The Names of God: Jehovah

Introduction:

Jehovah is the most common name of God in the Old Testament. It is used 6,823 times. It is often used in combination with Elohim and also in the same sentences with Elohim. It is not just another name for God, however, as it has a significance of its own.

I. **The Meaning of the Name**
   A. It is from the Hebrew word for "to be" or "to have being"
      1. "To be self-existent"
      2. "To possess essential life"
   B. Maimonides said, "All the names of God in Scripture are derived from His works except one, Jehovah; and this is called the 'plain name,' because it teaches plainly and unequivocally of the substance of God."

II. **The Manifestation of the Name**
   A. It was known as early as Genesis 2, but it was not fully revealed until Exodus 3
   B. It is the name usually used by God to reveal Himself to His people
   C. It had special significance to Moses
      1. "I am that I am" or "I will be what I will be"
      2. "I am . . . ."—Moses could fill in the blank on the basis of what he needed

III. **The Message of the Name**
   A. It reveals God as a God of moral and spiritual attributes
      1. Righteousness and holiness
      2. It has a strong note of justice also
   B. Its reveals God as a God of love
      1. His holiness must condemn
      2. His love provides redemption
   C. It reveals God as a God who seeks to restore
      1. Leviticus 1-7 deals with the system of sacrifice and uses "Jehovah" 86 times
      2. Most of His acts of restoration are as Jehovah

Conclusion:

From the earliest days, the name of Jehovah was taken as the embodiment of that hope for the human race which found expression in sacrifice and prayer. It is as Jehovah that God provides for our salvation.

The Names of God: Jehovah-M'Kaddesh

Leviticus 20:8

Introduction:
The term "sanctification" is often used. The name of God used here has to do with sanctification and reveals something special about our relationship to God.

I. **The Meaning**
   A. The usual: to be holy in the sense of freedom from sin
      1. That can't be all of the definition as:
         a. Days, places and things are sanctified; they are unrelated to sin
         b. We are called upon to "sanctify the Lord" (surely this is no sin to be put away in Him)
      2. We must look for further clarification
   B. The primary meaning is "to set apart, to differentiate, to stress the difference between"
      1. This is the essential meaning in regard to God, not His sinlessness but His differentness
      2. This explains how we can sanctify a day, a place, a thing, and even sanctify God
      3. Holiness in God first means, "difference from, set-apartness"

II. **The Explanation**
   A. "Set yourselves apart and view yourselves as different"
      1. Be different from the people around you
      2. View yourselves as different from the people around you
   B. "Because I have made you different"
      1. I have made you different, set you apart
      2. This is supported in the same chapter (and many other places)
         a. Verse 23: Be different from the nation around you
         b. Verse 24: I have separated you from others
         c. Verse 25: 1 have put a difference, separated between various things
         d. Verse 26: I have severed you from other people

III. **The Application**
   A. The Lord which sanctifies is the Lord who makes you different, sets you apart
      1. This is not a common interpretation
      2. We are set apart for Him, made different from the world by Him

3. This has both positive and negative aspects
   a. We are set apart to Him
   b. We are made different from the world
   B. This has many implications
      1. We are to be like Him
      2. We are to be different from the world in such things as perspective, value system, priorities, and point of reference
      3. Out of these differences arise our other differences, the things we don't do and the things we do

Conclusion:

The Lord which sanctifies is the Lord who sets us apart and makes us different. We are to view ourselves as different. We are to act differently. This includes the battle with sin, but it is a far bigger matter than that. The Lord wants us different; too bad we spend so much time trying to be like.

The Names of God: Adonai

Deuteronomy 10:17-20

Introduction:

People are interesting because there is an infinite variety of them. People are complex and different. God is even more interesting. He is infinitely complex in the truest sense, and that is why He has so many names. This passage treats the most common one. Note the things that can be found in this name that are significant.

I. **Sovereignty**
    A. Defined: "The name signifies ownership, mastery, indicating the truth that God is the owner of each member of the human family and that He consequently claims the unrestricted obedience of all."
    B. Illustrated: Deuteronomy 10:17-20, "Masters of Masters"; Malachi 1:6, "Master"; Acts 9:6, "Master"
    C. He is absolute sovereign over all creatures

II. **Sensitivity**
    A. The purchased slave was in a warm relationship (Exodus 12:43-45)
        1. The slave had the right of protection, help and direction (Psalm 123:2)
        2. The servant was heir (Genesis 15:1 & 2)
        3. Being the master required sensitivity (Deuteronomy 10:18 & 19)
    B. He is absolute sovereign, but He is not a harsh master in that sovereignty

III. **Surrender**
    A. Adonai requires surrender (Isaiah 6:1-8; Exodus 32:13)
    B. He is absolute sovereign. The only question is whether or not I recognize Him as such

IV. **Service**
    A. This is defined by such passages as Exodus 4:10; Deuteronomy 10:20b; John 13:13-16
    B. He is absolute sovereign. This must be recognized for the success of our service

Conclusion:

He is Lord. He is such a Lord that we need not be afraid of Him. He is such a Lord as to be owned. He is such a Lord as to require surrender in order to bless service. How do you relate to this Lord of Lords?

The Names of God: Jehovah-Rophe

Exodus 15:22-26

Introduction:

Bitterness is a major problem among Christians. Only God Himself knows the amount of damage that is done by this negative emotion.

I. **The Situation**
   A. They had crossed the Red Sea
   B. They had gone three days journey
   C. They had found no water

II. **The Crisis**
   A. They then found water
   B. They could not drink it because it was bitter
   C. This caused murmuring against Moses

III. **The Issue**
   A. The people murmured against Moses
      1. It was actually against God
      2. God saw their lack of faith
      3. This was a mark of folly in the light of the recent deliverance
   B. The waters weren't the only thing bitter
   C. Bitterness and lack of faith aways go together
      1. Bitterness at God because we won't believe His goodness
      2. Bitterness at circumstances because we don't believe His providence
      3. Bitterness at people because we don't believe His ability to handle them

IV. **The Answer**
   A. The tree cast into the water stands for the cross which sweetens the bitter
   B. God made a covenant with them
      1. "If thou wilt harken, do right, give ear, keep statutes"
      2. "I will put none of the diseases upon thee that have come upon thee"
      3. "I am the Lord that healeth"

V. **The Application**
   A. We can escape the plagues that come as a result of violating God's conditions
   B. He can heal bitterness through the cross

1. The bitterness of sin
2. Bitterness toward God
3. Bitterness toward circumstances as we are a special purchased possession
4. Bitterness toward others

Conclusion:

Bitterness is neither inescapable nor unavoidable. God has made provision to care for our bitterness just as He did for the children of Israel. Are you bitter?

The Names of God: Jehovah-Shalom

Judges 6:24

Introduction:

How would you feel if you were working out in your garden when . . .? Well, this is what happened to Gideon, and it makes quite a story.

I. **The Background of Jehovah-Shalom**
   A. Judges covers a time frame greater than American history to this point
   B. There are seven periods of trial and deliverance
   C. At this point, they were going through time of trial by the hand of the Midianites

II. **The Introduction of Jehovah-Shalom**
   A. Gideon: a common man with a common task
   B. A visitor comes and discusses his assignment
   C. He becomes aware that the man represents God
   D. Gideon was filled with fear
      1. He recognized the awesomeness of God
      2. He realized something of the holiness of God
   E. God gives Him reassurance in a specific word (23)
   F. Gideon builds an altar there
      1. Altars represent the place where God and man meet
      2. Altars were only rightly built in places of great spiritual experience

III. **The Meaning of Jehovah-Shalom**
   A. The Lord is my peace, or the Lord is at peace with me
   B. Gideon had three concerns at the moment:
      1. He had a specific problem: fear of immediate death
         a. No man could see God and live
         b. He expected to die
      2. He had a general problem of fear engendered by the sight of God
      3. He had external problems of great size awaiting him
   C. God met all of Gideon's concerns
      1. He told him he would not die
      2. He told him not even to be afraid
      3. He told him that He would give him peace
   D. This was what Gideon was memorializing

IV. **The Message of Jehovah-Shalom**
   A. We have the same types of concerns that faced Gideon
      1. Specific fears, etc.

      2. General unrest
      3. External difficulties
  B. We need the same message as Gideon
      1. God can solve our problems
      2. Only God can solve our problems
      3. The answers to our problems are internal and not in externals
      4. The answers to our problems are in our relationship to God
      5. We may need an encounter with God in order to find the answers

Conclusion:

Have you built an altar to Jehovah-Shalom? Do you even know who Jehovah-Shalom is? Are you looking for answers in places where you cannot possibly find them? The answer lies within, from the Lord, and it may be time for the experience that seals it.

Psalm 23

Introduction:

The twenty-third Psalm is probably the most familiar and best loved of all Scripture passages. Its main theme, the Lord as shepherd, illustrates this name of God.

I. **The Lord**
    A. The name identifies Who it is
    B. The name tells something of His character
        1. The God of the heavens
        2. The One Who is eternal
        3. The Holy One of Israel
        4. The Immutable One

II. **"Shepherd"**
      This develops the role and function of the shepherd:
    A. The shepherd leads
    B. The shepherd guides the errant
    C. The shepherd provides
    D. The shepherd protects
    E. The shepherd pursues
    F. The shephed restores the wanderer

III. **"My"**
    A. Note the personal nature of His relationship
    B. I can claim that for myself
        1. This takes truth from the realm of the theoretical
        2. This brings the eternal into touch with the temporal

IV. **"Is"**
    A. Is this actually true?
    B. Are you enjoying what is involved?

Conclusion:

The Shepherd-sheep relationship is one of the most precious in Scripture. Do you know it personally?

The Names of God: Jehovah-Tsidkenu

Jeremiah 23:1-6

Introduction:

There are many Bible characters I would like to change places with just to experience what they did. But not Jeremiah. He is known as the "weeping prophet." He just plain had it tough.

I. **His Placement**
    A. The background is the overall history of the divided kingdoms
    B. Israel had gone into Assyrian captivity 100 years before
    C. The land of Judah was full of evil
    D. This is the time to which God sent Jeremiah

II. **His Preaching**
    A. This section is part of larger context which begins with chapter 21.
    B. The meaning of the passage
        1. "Pastors" = kings
        2. The facts are in verses 1 & 2; the prediction is in verse 3 and following
        3. This does not refer to the return from captivity
        4. The Righteous Branch is on the same tree but in a different place on it
        5. The coming King shall be called Jehovah-Tsidkenu
        6. The big issue of the future shall be the regathering
    C. Jeremiah's message: condemnation now, but comfort for later

III. **His Prediction**
    A. He points to the coming captivity
    B. He predicts a new king on the throne of David
        1. He will actually reign
        2. His reign will be the realization of the perfection desired for David
    C. This king shall be called the "Lord our righteousness"
        1. He is none other than Christ
        2. This is none other than millenial rule
        3. The name: "The Lord who makes us righteous"

IV. **His Principles**
    A. God requires righteousness
        1. This is taught directly and implied throughout
        2. It is part of His holiness
    B. No man can attain to righteousness alone

1. All men are fatally flawed
2. All human systems fail at this point
C. Only Christ can provide righteouness
    1. He is the Lord who makes us righteous
    2. God has designed no other source
D. We are made righteous in Christ
    1. This comes through salvation
    2. This comes at time of salvation
E. We are then to develop righteousness
    1. Thus, no facade is provided for the unrighteous
    2. Righteousness now becomes a part of our essential character

Conclusion:

There is hope for us. God often moves in the darkest hour, and He will rule and reign. There is a challenge for us. We are righteous, we are to develop righteousness, and we are not to fall back on the righteousness of Christ as an excuse or cover.

The Names of God: Jehovah-Shammah

Ezekiel 48:35

Introduction:

Ezekiel saw the wheel, but that wasn't all he saw. He had two difficult tasks: First, to keep before the generation born in exile the way in which the nation had got there. Second, to sustain the faith of the exiles by promises of national restoration, justice, and future glory under the restored line of David. In the process, he uses the name of God—Jehovah-Shammah—in the last phrase of the very last prophecy in the very last chapter of the book.

I. The Meaning of the Term
   A. The translation—"Jehovah is there"
   B. The context
      1. He was speaking out of Israel's darkest time
      2. He was giving encouragement of future glory
      3. He was capping it all off with a promise of God's presence
   C. The implications
      1. God always gives hope in the darkest of times to keep His people going
      2. God would end the mess, and He will yet do so

II. The Truth in the Term
   A. God was with Israel in the Old Testament, especially in a visible sense from Exodus on
      1. At Mt. Sinai
      2. In the pillar of fire and cloud
      3. In the tabernacle and then the temple
   B. God was with man in Christ
   C. God is with man in his heart
   D. God will be with man in the millenium
   E. God will be with man (man will be with God) in eternity

III. The Importance of the Term
   A. His presence is a matter of comfort
      1. This is illustrated by the disciples in the storm
      2. No matter where you are or how bad the storm, He knows and He is there
   B. His presence is a matter of caution
      1. This is illustrated in Joshua 1:9
      2. No matter what the challenge, His presence will go with you

Conclusion:

The Lord is there. That is a comfort in trouble; draw on it. That is a caution when doing wrong; better get turned around. That is a challenge when faced with the unknown. If it is His will, you can do it. He has promised His presence, and you don't have to wait until the millenium or eternity to know it.

The Provision of God

Genesis 6:8-22

Introduction:

"There hath no temptation taken you but such as is common to man; but God is faithful, who will not suffer you to be tempted above that ye are able; but will with the temptation also make a way to escape, that ye may be able to bear it." 1 Corinthians 10:13. This verse has a lot to do with Noah. What has this to do with Noah?

I. **God Is Purposeful**
   A. The day of grace had run out
   B. The depth of sin was widespread
   C. God was ready to do something about it

II. **God Is Powerful**
   A. "I, even I" (verse 17)
   B. All that happened was a violation of God
   C. Always beware of God's power

III. **God Is Practical**
   A. He provides a workable means of escape
      1. Note just the general conception
      2. This was not a ship, but a great floating box
   B. He provides for the preservation of animals
      1. God rounded them up
      2. Were they docile, being aware of impending danger?
      3. We don't know how many species
      4. God made provision for sustenance
      5. It may have involved hibernation
   C. God provides for Noah's occupation and peace of mind

IV. **God Is Prescient**
   A. God always fully knows what is going on
   B. God always knows exactly what is needed to deal with every situation
   C. God always knows exactly what He's doing

V. **God Is Provident**
   A. He saw the righteousness of Noah
      1. He made provision to spare Him
      2. He made it worth being spared for
   B. He left room for Noah's responsibility
      1. It was absolutely crucial that Noah obey
      2. Verse 22 is the key to the passage

C. God promises to make a covenant with Noah

Conclusion:

All these things are still true of God and all are also personally true. Among other things, "Nothing just happens; it is planned." God always suits things to accomplish His ends in the best way possible. God knows all that will happen and that can happen.

God's Dealings

Introduction:

Noah was quite a man, but we are not told very much about him. That is good because we need to look at his God. As we review the story of Noah, we see how God deals with people.

I.   **Individually**
   A. His sons and their wives went with him
   B. It was based on Noah's faith
   C. It was likely through Noah's influence

II. **Discriminately (2 & 3, 8 & 9)**
   A. Notice the difference made between clean and unclean
   B. Notice the terminology used to describe
   C. God is always making differences
   D. Man is always trying to eliminate those differences

III. **Predeterminately (4)**
   A. God is the absolute authority
   B. God is completely faithful. Notice other 40 day periods: a period of trial terminating in the triumph of good or the overthrow of evil:
      1. Moses in the Mount
      2. Israel in the wilderness
      3. Elijah in flight
      4. Ninevah in probation
      5. Church in waiting

IV. **Objectively**
   A. We have no record of Noah's emotions as they don't figure in the mind of God
      1. We don't know everything
      2. Human emotions are not a valid test
   B. We can be glad God doesn't work on the basis of feelings, etc.
   C. We are usually subjective, not objective

V.   **Exclusively**
   A. Not one other person came into the ark
   B. There were probably 120 years between the promise and its fulfilment
   C. Man tries to generalize; God is exclusive

VI. **Caringly**
   A. "In the six hundredth year of Noah's life"

B. "The saints of the Lord . . . are so important in His eyes that time is reckoned according to their lives"

C. God was faithful to the faithful

VII. Intelligently

A. It was obviously a universal flood

B. God closed the door which took pressure off Noah both ways

Conclusion:

The God with whom we deal is of such greatness that we need to rethink our relationship to Him. Do we understand Him? Do we allow Him to be God? Do we obey Him? Do we trust Him?

The Goodness of God

Genesis 8

Introduction:

Isn't God good? No wonder we sing, "God is so good." His goodness is shown here in several special ways.

I.   He Remembers His Own (8:15-17)
   A.   The flood has now wound down
   B.   Everyone is safe who was promised safety

II.   He Is Easily Pleased (8:18-21a)
   A.   Noah offered a sacrifice
      1.   This is the reason for extra clean animals
      2.   It was doubtlessly out of gratitude
   B.   God "smelled a sweet savor" and was pleased
      1.   It doesn't take much to please God
      2.   This is contrary to common opinion

III.   He Preserves Life (9:1-8)
   A.   A series of prohibitions is given
      1.   Be fruitful
      2.   Instill fear in animals
      3.   Dietary limits are expanded
      4.   Blood is not allowed
      5.   A penalty is put on killing man
   B.   All these are designed to preserve man while he is replenishing the earth

IV.   He Provides for Needs
   A.   He recognizes man's situation (8:21b)
   B.   He promises no further destruction (8:21 & 22)
   C.   He provides human government (9:5 & 6)
   D.   He develops mercy
      1.   Genesis 3:16
      2.   Man is not to be wiped out again
      3.   He is promised a son
      4.   This leads to the final appearance of Christ

V.   He Gives Assurances (9:12-17)
   A.   He gives the sign of the rainbow
      1.   It was not necessarily new
      2.   It becomes a sign
      3.   The sign is right in what it threatens
   B.   This is typical of God's normal operations
      1.   He gives us assurances
      2.   He sometimes comes to us in the threat

Conclusion:

God is so good. We should respond to that goodness. If we don't, God has another side. We can do things willingly, or we can do them under duress. The sixteenth century martyr, Hugh Latimer, put it well when he said:

"We must first be made good, before we can do good; we must first be made just, before our works can please God.—for when we are justified by faith in Christ, then come good works."

God Who Demands Obedience

Genesis 11:26-12:5

Introduction:

Just think of poor Sarah. Your husband comes home one night and says that you are moving. He has no idea exactly where you are going. He doesn't even know how you are getting there. Sarah put up with a lot from that man. It seems God spoke to him and told him he was to make the move. Abraham did what God told him, and Sarah managed to bring it all off.

I. God Requires Complete Obedience
A. His Word is always to be obeyed
B. Even when
    1. A thing is clearly impossible
    2. A course is totally unfamiliar
    3. A destination is completely unclear

II. God Rewards the Obedient Person
A. He gave Abraham a seven-fold blessing
B. Most of God's commands have built-in blessing as well as reasons given
C. We must obey regardless of the reward, but we can be sure of ultimate reward

III. God Reserves the Highest Place for the Obedient
A. Note the chronology of Abram and Terah
    1. Terah had children at 70 (11:26)
    2. He died at 205 (11:32)
    3. Abram was 75 when he left Haran (12:4)
    4. The years involved don't total up
B. The possible solutions
    1. There is a mistake in the numbers (this is possible, but it is neither likely nor necessary)
    2. Abraham may have been the youngest child
    3. He may have left before his father's death
    4. This can mean, "when his father was dead to him"
C. Lesson: Obedience to the Word of God takes precedence over all

IV. God Reviews Our Obedience
A. God calls upon us to obey
B. He then
    1. Doesn't always show us how things will end
    2. Doesn't always make things go smoothly
    3. Doesn't always preserve us from problems

C. God sometimes tests our willingness before He works things out or gives us the promised blessing

Conclusion:

What is God showing you from the Word? Where is your problem? Why will you not do what the Bible says? Won't you begin doing so right now? We need to commit to doing what the Bible says and trusting God to bring things out right. Will you do that?

God the Rewarder of Right

Genesis 13:5-18

Introduction:

Abram had just returned from Egypt, back into fellowship with God. Now something else significant is about to happen. This passage appears to be two stories, but it actually is all one.

I. God Ministers to Us at Difficult Times

A. It must have been a hard time for Abram
1. The strife over pasturage
2. The separation from Lot (they had been together quite a while)

B. It is more than coincidental that God speaks just now (v. 14)

C. God ministers to us at these difficult times too, but we often miss what He is doing
1. We are eaten up over what is happening
2. We are concentrating on what we appear to have lost
3. We are wanting other than what God is in the process of giving us

II. God Always Rewards Right

A. Abram had done what he believed was right
1. He had been rewarded by Lot with selfishness
2. Now God will set the record straight

B. God gives Him an incredible reward
1. He adds to the promise already given
2. He sends him off to "check it out"
3. Lot got the paradise; Abram got the promise

C. These are important and comforting thoughts
1. God keeps the records
2. God promises to right all the wrong

D. We must maintain, "right is its own reward," because some rewards only come after this life is over
1. We don't need to worry about this kind of thing
2. We need to concentrate on ourselves and not worry about others

III. God Doesn't Think As We Think

A. Abram's action runs contrary to common sense and current "pop psych"
1. He made no effort to look out for himself
2. He obviously did the right thing

B. This points up that God thinks differently

1. We see what appears; He sees what is
2. We see what is in process; He sees how it will conclude
3. We see the limits; God sees the expanse
C. This is very instructive
    1. It shows—almost as an aside—the importance of faith
    2. It shows us the importance of living by the Bible in our daily lives
    3. It teaches us to expect to be "out of sync" with the world around us

Conclusion:

The God of Abram is our God today. He comes to us in our difficulties. He rewards right even though we may not see it. He doesn't think as we think. We need to take the New Testament challenge of coming to think as God does so we can find things in His Word and pattern after them.

Knowing God

Genesis 15:1-21

Introduction:

Abram knew a lot about God. He knew what He was like. He knew how He operated. He knew what He demanded and expected, but there was something else that he needed to know and that was God Himself. This chapter is the story of Abram really getting to know God.

I. **He Needed to Know God As His Source**
   A. We can trace his rescue of Lot
   B. In this he had done two things
      1. He angered powerful kings
      2. He had passed up an opportunity for gain
   C. God assures him that He would supply in those areas of need, and he needed to hear God say, "I am all you need"

II. **He Needed to Know God As His Guarantor (2-5)**
   A. "What good will it do me to have such?"
      1. This is a question of confusion, not of challenge
      2. It becomes an expression of fact
   B. He Gets a direct answer from God
      1. One born of you will be heir
      2. God said, "You will have much more than that one," and he needed to hear God say, "I always keep my promises"

III. **He Needed to Know God As His Savior (6)**
   A. This is a classic passage
      1. Abram believed what God told him
      2. God declared him in right standing as a result
   B. This shows two important truths:
      1. It defines Old Testament salvation
      2. He did nothing to earn his salvation
   C. Abram learned that God is Savior; salvation is entirely of Him, and he needed to hear God say, "I have provided for your salvation"

IV. **He Needed to Know God As Good (7-11; 17-21)**
   A. God commanded a strong action
      1. It was the way to "cut a covenant"
      2. It is rich in symbolism
   B. Note the difference between a covenant and a contract
      1. This was a covenant
      2. It involves God giving without anything coming to him in return

C. This stresses that God gives regardless of what man does, and he needs to hear God say, "Your best interest is my eternal concern"

V. He Needed to Know God As Provident (12-16)
    A. God traced the family history in advance
        1. He told him of the "Horror of great darkness"
        2. This showed what they would go through
        3. God had two purposes:
           a. His timing was not ready
           b. Things needed to be done to them
    B. God made it plain that He knew how it would turn out before it even started
        1. He knew because He controlled it
        2. He is fully in charge and Abram needed to hear God say, "I control everything so I know how it is going to come out"

Conclusion:
Abram knows a lot about God, what God is like, how He operates, and what He expects. Now he simply needed to know God. We are like Abram and simply need to know God. We come to know Him by allowing the Holy Spirit to interpret His self-revelation to our hearts.

God's Self-Revelation

Genesis 18

Introduction:

Revelation is something like a megaphone. More information is given as the story progresses. This is nowhere more obvious than in the life of Abraham. He gets more information as his story moves along.

I. **"Is Anything Too Hard for the Lord?" (14)**
   - A. The exchange
     1. Information is given in Sarah's hearing
     2. Her response is laughter
     3. A rebuke comes
     4. She lies, and God corrects it
   - B. The principle: there is nothing that is too hard for God
   - C. The response desired
     1. God wanted faith from her—there is nothing too hard for God, especially something that He has promised
     2. God desires faith from us—there is nothing too hard, especially if He has promised it in His Word.

II. **"For I Know Him" (19)**
   - A. The exchange
     1. God speaks of sharing with Abraham
     2. God gives him significant information
   - B. The principle: God desires simple obedience in the everyday things of life
   - C. The response desired
     1. God simply desires Abraham to do right and to command his family to do so also
     2. This, rather than some spectacular thing, defines "good Christianity"
     3. God desires our everyday obedience

III. **"Shall Not The Judge of All the Earth Do Right?" (25)**
   - A. The exchange
     1. Abraham is pleading with God
     2. He raises the question more for himself than for God
     3. This is part of the conviction process
   - B. The principle: Surely God does that which is right
     1. The "cry" of Sodom and Gomorrah—"sin is very grievous"
     2. "I will go down . . . and see . . ."
     3. God allows intercession

C. The response desired
    1. Abraham needed confidence that what God would do was right
    2. God was teaching him that he could trust God Himself
    3. God desires confidence from us
        a. This is the point at which we have enormous problems if things don't go as we think they should
        b. "Confidence"—absolute assurance that He knows what He is doing

Conclusion:

God expects us to walk before Him in sincerity. God desires us to show faith, obedience and confidence. Are you passing His test?

God Is

Introduction:

The Bible is full of great men and great themes, but the greatest person and theme of all is God. We get a tremendous view of God here, and we see eight things about Him.

I. **He Is the God of the Valleys (23:1 & 2)**
    A. This is a dark point in Abraham's life
    B. It shows that no matter what your heartache or grief, God is there

II. **He Is the God of the Pilgrim Pathway (23:4)**
    A. Two statements are made about Abraham
        1. "Stranger"—one living out of his own country
        2. "Sojourner"—one dwelling in a land in which he is not naturalized
    B. These are explained in Hebrews 11:13
    C. We must remember that we are pilgrims

III. **He Is the God of Real People (23:4-20)**
    A. The story is true to the customs of the time
        1. Haggling (6,11,13 & 15)
        2. Intercessors (8)
        3. Weighing out payment (16)
        4. A deed (17)
        5. An oath (24:2)
    B. We do not deal with vague, hazy, and shadowy people, but with real live ones, people to whom you and I can relate

IV. **He Is a God of Proper Procedure (23:15 &16)**
    A. In spite of all the customs involved, He still follows through to a conclusion
    B. He kept Abraham from being obligated to the ungodly
    C. Not only is what we do important, but the way in which we do it is also
    D. God is a God of proper procedure!

V. **He Is a God of Answered Prayer (24:12-14)**
    A. Entrusted with great responsibility, Abraham prays
    B. He seeks specific direction which is not necessarily wrong if done with a right motive
    C. His prayer is answered almost before he is finished praying

VI. He Is a God of Specific Guidance (24:27)—Abraham's servant speaks
   A. "I being in the way" (going about my proper business)
   B. "The Lord led me"

VII. He Is a God of Wondrous Provision (24:15,28,49-51,55-56, 58)
   A. Everything necessary for the fulfillment of God's will was wondrously worked out
   B. God always perfects His provision and provides that which is best for His child

VIII. He Is a God of Perfected Purposes (24:61-67)
   A. It was a common custom to get a wife this way
   B. He brought complete harmony to the situation
   C. When God works things out (and is allowed to do so) they always come out perfectly

Conclusion:
   Take heart in a dark day. God is working and will work until He is finished. Remember He said, "Lo I am with you always, even unto the end."

God's Tests

Genesis 26:1-5

Introduction:

Isaac is not mentioned often in Scripture. Most mentions are in conjunction with someone else. Where he does show, he comes through very well. There are only two occasions where God spoke to him in any direct manner. One was a time of testing—"There was famine in the land." This shows us some very valuable things about how God works in times of testing.

I. **God Usually Shows Himself Somewhere in the Time of Testing**
    A. He comes and speaks to Isaac here
    B. He usually comes to us as well, but we often miss it because we are so busy fussing about the testing, etc.

II. **God's Promises Are Not Diminished by the Problems Encountered While Being Tested**
    A. Isaac had been promised the land
        1. The famine in the land raised questions
        2. God came with assurances
    B. Any promise we have is not altered by the problems that may come before it is fulfilled

III. **God Suits His Testings to the Character and Strength of His Children**
    A. Note the different directions
        1. God left Abraham to determine himself
        2. God told Isaac not to go down
        3. God later told Jacob to go (Genesis 46:3 & 4)
    B. Assuming that Egypt is a place of trial and exercise for His people, we see how God tailors tests to His people's characters.
        1. Abraham: a man of high attainment and close communication with God. All places were alike for him
        2. Isaac: a good man not cut out for hardship
        3. Jacob: a strong man accustomed to difficult times and hardships
    C. God always suits His tests to His people
        1. He always takes needs into account
        2. He also considers character and ability
        3. This is why He can say we are not tempted beyond our ability

IV. **God's Presence in Testing Enables Us Not Only to Go But Also to Stay Anywhere**
   A. We know that we can go anywhere with Him
   B. It is equally true that we can stay anywhere ("If Jesus is with me, I'll stay anywhere")
   C. When God is testing, we need to stay in some of the difficult places for His will to be perfected

V. **God's Promises Are Provided for Our Stay in Times of Testing**
   A. The deeper the trial, the greater the need to remind ourselves of the promise
   B. "Those that must live by faith have need often to review and repeat to themselves the promises that they are to live upon, especially when they are called to any instance of suffering."

VI. **God's Promises Are Secured Through Our Obedience**
   A. Notice all the terms used of Abraham in verse 5. They indicate the full extent of his faith; he believed God enough to act on His commandments and accept His promises
   B. God often has one of two related purposes in our testing:
      1. To try our faith
      2. To determine our obedience
   C. We can be sure of receiving the promises when we determine to obey

Conclusion:

Isaac found how God works in times of testing. Will you accept His operation through your times of trial?

The Self-Existence of God

Exodus 3:1-4

Introduction:

Moses was introduced to God's name—"I AM THAT I AM." We say, "I am what I am . . ." God is that He is—absolutely self-existent. What does that mean?

I.   **God Is Untraceable**
  A. We trace all things through cause and effect
  B. God is the ultimate first cause as He has no origin
    1. He always was
    2. There is nothing more to say than, "in the beginning, God"

II. **God Is Unknowable**
  A. We have no regular sources of knowledge in regard to God
    1. We know men by other men, but there is no other god to know Him by
    2. We know men by their ancestors, but God has none
  B. This is a major problem of science
    1. It is challenging to say, "We don't know"
    2. It is humiliating to say, "We can't know"
  C. All we know of God is what He has chosen to reveal
    1. There are three sources of revelation: nature, human consciousness, Scripture
    2. Two of these are adversely affected by the fall and sin
    3. The Bible is the only accurate, trustworthy source we have

III. **God Is Unchallengeable**
  A. God is under no obligation to reveal or explain Himself to anyone
    1. He has chosen to reveal and explain some certain things
    2. There is much He has chosen to keep in the counsels of His own will
  B. This fact demands a change in our attitude and philosophy
    1. If God is good and
    2. He is under no obligation to reveal/expain anything
    3. Then we really have no business questioning Him

Conclusion:

Our humanistic society has rubbed off on us, and we have problems with God. We don't like the way He does some things and we think He is obligated to explain things. It is arrogant to question

God; it is even more arrogrant to question God without any knowledge of the Bible (which most who question lack). We've lost the fear of the Lord because we have lost a God worthy of fear.

In reply to the query: "Why is there but one God?" a little girl replied: "Because God fills every place, and there's no room for another one." Oh, that our faith was as simple and straightforward as hers!

The God of the Burning Bush

Exodus 3:1-5

Introduction:

It is a singular fact, but Joseph did not have one direct encounter with God. Moses had repeated ones. Moses wanted to see God through encounters, and he illustrates four truths.

I. God Has a Specific Detailed Plan for Moses's Life
   A. Note the details recorded here
   B. Note the divisions of his life's flow
   C. Note the interplay between the parts of his life
   D. God has a plan for every life

II. God Knew Exactly Where Moses Was
   A. He was in a remote place
   B. He was not in
      1. The place where he started
      2. The place where he wanted
      3. The place where he was suited
   C. He was doing what was his to do
   D. God knows where you are, no matter where or what

III. God Arrested Moses's Attention
   A. He used a unique means
   B. God spoke with an audible voice, but revelation is complete in our day
   C. God seeks to arrest our attention
      1. He uses a variety of unique things
      2. He wants our attention:
         a. To correct something
         b. To lead us on to something else
      3. We ignore His attempts at our own loss

IV. God Helped Moses with His Perspective
   A. He forced him to recognize His holiness
   B. His actions were designed to bring home the difference
   C. He clearly identified who he was
   D. God still reminds us of perspective
      1. We live in a flippant day
      2. We have lost our sense of awe
      3. We need a fresh dose of the fear of God

Conclusion:

You can count on the fact that God has a plan for your life and knows where you are. Are you heeding the burning bushes? Do you have an adequate sense of His Holiness?

God's Assurances

Exodus 5:22-6:30

Introduction:

Have you ever felt things couldn't get worse? That can be a trying time. It can also be an exciting time.

I. **God's Opportunity**
    A. The situation
        1. Pharaoh's arrogance was at its peak
        2. Hebrew despondence was total
        3. Moses's discomfiture was intense
        4. God's seeming indifference was overwhelming
    B. God's opportunity
        1. This is the way God often works
        2. "Man's extremity is God's opportunity"
    C. The reasons:
        1. To make God obvious
        2. To force man to trust
        3. To teach the adequacy of His assurances
    D. The meaning
        1. "You have no need until you have a need"
        2. The darkest times are thus encouraging

II. **God's Operation**
    A. God's awareness
        1. God knows what is going on
        2. God *really* knows what is going on
    B. God's authority
        1. He is absolutely able to act
        2. The only questions are, "Will He and when?"
    C. God's assurances
        1. His character (2 & 3)
        2. His covenant (4)
        3. His compassion (5)
        4. His condescension (6 & 8)
        5. His commitments (7)
    D. God's demand: He is determined that we should believe His Word, for that alone is sufficient in every situation

III. **God's Opposition**
    A. The Hebrews (9)
        1. They were too taken with their trouble to heed
        2. They were too cast down with disappointment to believe. "Strong passions oppose strong consolations"

43

     3. They were too devastated to act. "Disconsolate spirits often stand in their own light"

B. Moses
     1. He was overhelmed by the unlikelihood of Pharaoh hearing
     2. He was overwhelmed by the unreadiness of his own ability. Our infirmities ought to make us humble and dependent, but they should not stop us.

Conclusion:

God's assurances are designed to be enough. He wants us to accept and act on them. When things can't get worse, it is a good time for us to look for deliverance. Unfortunately, we tend to oppose God most at those times.

The Sovereignty of God
Exodus 14

Introduction:

How big is God? He is big enough to be the sovereign of the universe. He is big enough to be sovereign over all its affairs. Note how this story shows His sovereignty.

I. **He Is Sovereign in His Management**
  A. Moses
    1. He is meek but also weak and flawed
    2. He has shown his flaws and will show them again
  B. Pharaoh
    1. His besetting sin of pride was never dealt with
    2. God breaks and avenges Himself (God will be the loser to no man)
  C. Israel
    1. The nation has an incredible impact on all history
    2. At this point it is the sorry lot of "sad sacks" (11 & 12)

II. **He Is Sovereign in His Movement**
  A. One time He acts; another time He doesn't
    1. He always has a broader picture than we do
    2. He is not wholly predictable
  B. He moves in strong directions
    1. The situation of Israel here
    2. He moved into an impossible situation
    3. All this was part of a larger purpose

III. **He Is Sovereign in His Motives**
  A. We know what motivates God
    1. His own holiness (self-consistency)
    2. The welfare of His people
  B. We don't always know which
    1. One motive may overpower another
    2. He always acts out of motive (there are always reasons for the things He does)

IV. **He Is Sovereign in His Moments**
  A. He chooses when to act
    1. Sometimes He tolerates long
    2. Sometimes He acts suddenly
  B. Every action is "in the fulness of time"
  C. Every action here is "just in the nick of time" and just at the right moment

V. He Is Sovereign in His Methods
  A. He does His work in a variety of ways
    1. He could have walked on water
    2. He could have moved in other ways
  B. He tells the children of Israel to move, and He works through Moses
    1. He can work without men
    2. He usually works through us
  C. Note the details here
    1. The function of the pillar of cloud—to protect
    2. Note the dead bodies

Conclusion:

God is sovereign. He is aware of what is going on, knowledgeable about what He is doing, intelligent in His assignment of men, operating on the purest of motives, and moving at exactly the right time. We ought to reverence Him, have confidence in Him, submit to Him. Have you submitted and are you living so?

Let God Be God

Exodus 19:9-25

Introduction:

We are all about people; the Bible is all about God. We focus on prosperity, well-being, success; the Bible simply focuses on God. This passages mentions Him eighteen times and tells us seven things about Him.

I. God Expressed Himself (9)
A. He spoke to Moses
B. He spoke from a cloud
   1. This enabled Him to come close enough to be heard without being seen
   2. The cloud prevented curious inquiries into hidden secrets, but it pointed up the glory of what was revealed

II. God Elevated His Servant (9)
A. He put great honor on Moses
B. He caused the people to believe in him
C. This was because Moses was His messenger

III. God Exhibited His Method
A. It is always obedience first and then revelation
   1. John 7:17—"He that willeth to do . . . shall know"
   2. This is a uniform pattern
B. We really want to reverse this (we want things from God all out of proportion to our relationship to Him)

IV. God Emphasized Holiness (10, 14, 15)
A. Two days were given for preparation
B. "Sanctify them," call them off from their worldly business
C. Let them be ready. There are two signs of readiness:
   1. Washing of clothes
   2. Abandoning even lawful enjoyments (15)

V. God Entreated Reverence (12, 13, 21)
A. He set boundaries around the mountain
   1. This shows that man is not on the same plane as God
   2. At that point the distance was set between man and God
B. When the trumpet sounds, come and sit silently at the feet of God

VI. God Exalted His Message
A. Everything here is designed to draw attention to Him
   1. The thunder and lightning

2. The thick cloud
3. The trumpet blast
4. The fire and smoke
5. The trembling of the mountain
   B. He drew attention to Himself to point up His message

VII. God Exposed the People (21-24)
   A. He called Moses up and sent him back down
   B. He sent him to warn the people:
      1. Not to force their way through
      2. Not to come unconsecrated
   C. Moses said that such violation was impossible
   D. God knew the people for what they were

Conclusion:

God was dim, distant, detailed, demanding. The people were totally unresponsive. God is no longer dim but clear; distant but near; detailed but general; demanding but meets His own demands. But we still struggle wanting to do things our own way and wanting to do as little as possible for Him.

The Dark Side of God?

Exodus 20:5 & 6

Introduction:

God says that we are to have no other gods before His face. Two reasons are given why we should obey: 1) God is a jealous God and 2) God visits the iniquity of the fathers on the children. Both reasons appear very negative and need a closer look.

I. **The Jealousy of God**
   A. The modern word has negative connotation: "resentfully envious or suspicious of a rival or a rival's influence"
   B. The original word was neutral: "very watchful in guarding or keeping; requiring exclusive loyalty"
   C. God's jealousy is positive
      1. He is defensive, protective of His uniqueness, sovereignty, ability, and character
      2. A God "beside" or an image undermines this by implying that God can be reduced to my level
   D. He clearly states that He will not share His glory with another
      1. He will not suffer a rival near His throne
      2. "For I the Lord Your God Am God Who brooks (or tolerates) no rival"—Berkley
      3. When attempts are made:
         a. He will strike down that "other"
         b. He will withdraw His blessing
   E. Beware of raising any person or thing to the level He alone should occupy
      1. He will withdraw His blessing
      2. He will strike the idol down

II. **Transgenerational Treatment of Sin**
   A. When another God is raised, His jealousy is stirred with the result that the sins of the fathers are visited upon the children for three or four generations
   B. Does this then mean that:
      1. Children are punished for their father's sins?
      2. Children are condemned to their father's sins?
   C. The meaning is important as it is often restated (Exodus 34:7; Numbers 14:18; Deuteronomy 5:9)
   D. It cannot mean that children are punished for their father's sins (Deuteronomy 24:16; Ezekiel 18:20)
   E. What does it mean?
      1. "Bringing home to the children . . . the sins of the fathers."

2. The children of idolators are more likely to be idolators, and the children of the godly are more likely to be godly
3. This is illustrated by the difficulty of reaching those subjected to family inbreeding and by the fact that Christianity tends to run in families (verse 6)

III. Applications

A. Beware of idolatry—it may come back to haunt you
B. There is a broader application: beware of what you do to your children:
   1. They will be responsible
   2. You will bear some of the blame

Conclusion:

Our God is a jealous God. He does not share His glory. He will topple any other god. He will withdraw His blessing from idolatrous people. Our God is a judging God. One of His most frightening methods is to let natural tendencies roll on unchecked.

His Name in Vain

Exodus 20:7

Introduction:

Most of us are free of many violations of the Ten Commandments. Christians don't usually murder or build actual idols. We like to think we are free of using His name in vain, but we usually are not. There are various ways in which we take His name in vain.

I. Profanity
A. This invokes God:
1. To do what we don't want done
2. To do what He never does
B. This debases deity
1. It is commonplace
2. It attributes to God what He doesn't do
3. It contributes to ill feeling about God

II. Perjury
A. It is naming the name of God and then lying
1. Includes false swearing
2. This is actually involved any time a Christian lies
B. There are few things that violate the command like lying
1. It associates God with what He cannot do
2. It wrongly identifies Him

III. Pretense
A. Prayer without practice
B. Practice without prayer
C. Giving without spirit
D. Worship without heart
E. Claiming the name verbally and denying it in life

IV. Profession
A. It includes making decisions on one's own and then attributing them to God
B. It includes making decisions without considering Him or His will
C. It includes claiming His Name openly, but denying Him in life

Conclusion:

Using the name of God in vain involves far more than profanity. "The man who never mentions the name of God is more likely clean than the man who is always talking about Him while denying Him in life." Would you be happy to have others use your name in the same way you use the name of God?

Utterly Awesome

Deuteronomy 4:9-14

Introduction:

Israel was ready to enter the land, and Moses was reviewing his significant teaching. He had reviewed, "Leave God's Word Alone." Now he reviews, "Learn to fear the Lord."

I. **What Is the "Fear of the Lord"?**
    A. This is a frequently repeated Old Testament concept
    B. It is best defined by the Sinai Experience
        1. Exodus 19:9-13, 16, 18-20
        2. Exodus 20:18-20
    C. It means reverential awe (it has an element of terror, but that is not the dominant influence)
    D. It is necessary because of our contrary natural tendency (Exodus 19:21-24)

II. **Why Did God Want Men to Fear Him?**
    A. So that they would obey His commandments
        1. The Ten Commandments
        2. The teaching that arises out of them
    B. Reverential awe should make us slower to challenge God
        1. It had small effect on Israel
        2. This answers questions about the intensity and severity of God's judgments
        3. He was awesome enough for them

III. **What Is the State of the Fear of the Lord Today?**
    A. It is best described by Psalm 36:1
    B. The New Testament has a different relationship between man and God so there is a different emphasis
        1. It is common to say that the aspect of terror is out of the picture
        2. Actually the terror is only less prominent
    C. The New Testament still makes a case for the fear of the Lord
        1. It is commanded of Christians (1 Peter 2:17)
        2. We are to live in the light of it (1 Peter 1:17)
        3. We are to be concerned with service because of it (Hebrews 12:28)
        4. We are to submit in the light of it (Ephesians 5:21)
        5. We are to perfect holiness motivated by it (2 Corinthians 7:1)
        6. We are to win souls inspired by it (2 Corinthians 5:11)

Conclusion:

This is the message of Luke 12:4 & 5. We need to develop some fear of the Lord in our arrogant, modern day. We need to stand in awe of Him because of what He has done and because of what He can do.

> There are four great impelling motives that move men to action: Fear, Hope, Faith, and Love—these four, but the greatest of these is Fear. Fear is first in order, first in force, first in fruit. Indeed, fear is "the beginning of wisdom." Scripture summarizes the chief cause of sin and crime: "There is no fear of God before their eyes."
>
> —*The Prairie Overcomer*

No Similitude

Deuteronomy 4:15-28

Introduction:

The Air Force Academy chapel illustrates an important historical truth. The comparative simplicity of the Jewish area reminds us of how well the Jews learned Moses's teaching regarding the making of idols.

I. **What Is Forbidden?**
   A. Why do we have the second commandment? (Exodus 20:3-5a)
      1. The first and the second are inseparable
      2. The first leads to the second; the second causes the first
   B. What is really forbidden?
      1. "Thou shalt not make"
      2. This includes
         a. Representing God by making images
         b. Worshiping images
         c. Worshiping God through images
      3. It does not even allow for any "intention"

II. **Why Is It Forbidden?**
   A. Because it undermines the spiritual aspect of God (it tries to portray an infinite spirit by a finite likeness)
   B. Because it undermines His status as Creator
      1. It tries to portray the great Creator by a mere creation
      2. It detracts from His grandeur
      3. It gives the glory that belongs to Him to something else
   C. Because it goes against specific biblical teaching
   D. Because it erodes the whole basis of faith
      1. Faith is based on the unseen
      2. "Faith cometh by . . ."
      3. It actually destroys what it seeks to assist
   E. Because it is so easy to transfer from what is represented to the object used to represent it

III. **What Difference Does It Make?**
   A. "There may be idols in the heart where there are none in the sanctuary"
   B. We have developed an intangible set of idols:
      1. People
      2. Professionals

3. Practices (lifestyle)
4. Positions (personal positions/opinions)
5. Possessions
6. Passions

IV. What Is the Danger?
A. That of suffering loss
  1. Losing the reality of our religion
  2. Losing God's blessing
B. That of being turned over to such gods as we have set up (verse 28)
  1. If you find satisfaction, then . . .
  2. We depend in need on what we depend indeed
C. That of becoming like them (Psalm 115:8)
  1. Our object of worship molds us after itself
  2. Is this why so few Christians finish well?

Conclusion:
Idolatry is a very serious sin. Some of the worst idolators, however, have no graven images. Are you an idolator?

Divine Rights

Psalm 24:1-6

Introduction:

There is a great fascination with monarchy. Monarchies are based on the divine right of kings. The only real divine rights are truly Divine rights.

I. **The Facts Stated**
   A. The earth is the Lord's
   B. The fullness thereof is the Lord's
      1. What is produced from the earth
      2. The control of nature
   C. The world is the Lord's
      1. Actually, "ecology, environment"
      2. Much environmental concern is correct but misdirected
   D. They that dwell therein are the Lord's
      1. All inhabitants, humans included
      2. All owe existence to Him

II. **The Facts Supported**
   A. The structure of Hebrew poetry
      1. Parallelism here
      2. Both phrases say the same thing
   B. We are dealing here with creation
      1. He has created all categories
      2. He has certain "creation rights"

III. **The Facts Strengthened**
   A. He has a right to establish a standard
      1. Implied by the question in v. 3
      2. As Creator He has the right to control His creation
   B. He has established the standard
      1. He has clearly done so (verse 4)
         a. Clean hands—proper actions
         b. Pure heart—proper inner self
         c. Not involved in vanity
         d. Not involved in untruthfulness
      2. He has the right to and actually has established the standard
   C. He has provided for the standard
      1. The person who qualifies receives from God
      2. God's provision includes
         a. Blessing from the Lord
         b. Righteousness from God
      3. This describes those who seek Him

IV. The Facts Simplified
- A. A small matter, the tithe
  1. The tithe is the Lord's
  2. There is a dual claim
     - a. All belongs to Him
     - b. It is part of the standard He has the right to set
- B. A larger matter, His commandments
  1. He has a right to set standards
  2. He has set standards
- C. The largest matter, your salvation
  1. He has determined the way
  2. He has provided the way
     - a. You can "receive" righteousness
     - b. You can be able to say, "God of my Salvation"

Conclusion:
Anything we bring to God is already His. Any demand He makes on us is right and proper. Any claim He makes is inescapable.

The Perfection of God

Psalm 138:8

Introduction:

We say, "It's a sure thing!" But there is almost nothing of which that is really true. Life is tremendously uncertain. The only things we can be sure of are spiritual. David was very sure of some things:

I.   **The Lord Is Working in My Life**
    A. God knows and controls all that happens
    B. God's working goes on at all times
        1. "The steps of a good man . . ."
        2. "I will instruct thee and teach . . ."
    C. Thus God does for me
        1. The things that I cannot do for myself
        2. The things that I will not do for myself

II. **The Lord Has Purpose in What He Does**
    A. He has a plan worked out which includes:
        1. A final product
        2. A particular course
    B. That plan is tailored to me
        1. There is none like it anywhere else
        2. It is suited to my tastes, needs, personality, etc.
    C. That plan is ultimately for my good
        1. It is for perfect good
        2. It is to make me what God wants me to be

III. **The Lord Will Fulfill His Work in Me**
    A. He will complete His work:
        1. In my present and future
        2. In those whom my life touches
        3. In those who will come after me
    B. He will perfectly make perfect His perfection
    C. He will keep on working in those in whom He has begun working

Conclusion:

What does it all mean to me? Everything that comes into my life is part of God's working in it. The less resistance I make, the less suffering I face. He won't stop working until He is finished. This is both frightening and encouraging. If you don't know Him, God is already working in your life. Why not open your life to His work?

Like a Shepherd

Isaiah 40:11

Introduction:

"There is probably only one thing dumber than a sheep and that is a man." Let's explore what that statement means.

I. **The Likeness of the Shepherd**
   A. It is frequently repeated in Scripture
   B. It is done to make the relationship understandable
   C. It covers various areas. The shepherd:
      1. Loves the sheep
      2. Guides the sheep
      3. Guards the sheep
      4. Feeds the sheep
      5. Gathers the sheep
      6. Cares for the sheep

II. **The Work of the Shepherd**
   A. He feeds the flock
      1. He does not force-feed them (even though some prefer it that way)
      2. He does not eat for them (although some are always angry because he does not)
      3. He does provide the context for them to feed themselves
         a. The table is spread for you
         b. How much do you eat on your own?
   B. He gathers the flock
      1. The word has the sense of "regathers"
      2. He is always seeking to call back those who will listen to Him
   C. He cares for the flock
      1. He knows the abilities of each sheep
      2. He suits His care to those needs
      3. The care is there; we sometimes won't accept the care He offers

III. **The Designations of the Shepherd**
   A. The "good" shepherd (John 10:11-14) is used in connection with salvation
   B. The "great" shepherd (Hebrews 13:20) is used in connection with resurrection
   C. The "chief" shepherd (1 Peter 5:4) is used in connection with the second coming

Conclusion:

Sheep aren't very bright. Sheep desperately need a shepherd. Men aren't even as bright. They have a shepherd and don't pay any attention. He feeds them, He regathers them, He cares for them, and they fight Him all the way. Stop fighting your shepherd.

Not all shepherds were *good* shepherds (John 10:11). A man whose thoughts were constantly in the cities and who loved noisy society hardly found pleasure in lonely places where sheep were his only companions. Throughout the ministry of Jesus, He constantly referred to His followers as sheep, and frequently affirmed that His audiences were as sheep without a shepherd (Mark 6:34). There were certain unmistakable characteristics of all good shepherds. They loved their sheep, enjoyed their company, and were willing to sacrifice much to protect them from enemies. David, the shepherd boy, killed wild animals in order to defend his flock (1 Samuel 17:17:34-36). The shepherd led his sheep to green pasture and thus provided their food. Without his aid, the sheep would die; without their company, the shepherd's life would be exceedingly lonely. Jesus was mindful of all these details when He said, "I am the good shepherd."

—*Ivor Powell*

Our Incomparable God

Isaiah 40:18,25; 46:5

Introduction:

We constantly deal in comparisons, but such comparisons break down in relationship to God. "To whom will you liken God?" "What likeness will you compare to Him?" "To whom shall God be equal?" "To whom can we compare God to make a likeness?" The Prophet brings us face to face with realities.

I. We Can't Compare God to Anything or Anyone (12)
   A. Likenesses are possible and illustrative
   B. Comparisons are impossible
       1. To the ocean? (He can hold all moisture in His hand)
       2. To the heavens? (He measures the heavens by the ruler in His hand)
       3. To the earth? (He puts the dust in a measure)
       4. To the mountains? (He holds the scales that weigh the mountains)

II. We Can't Understand God (13 & 14)
   A. We can only *know* Him as He reveals Himself in
       1. Conscience
       2. The natural world
       3. The Word of God
   B. This says nothing about understanding Him (Isaiah 55:8 & 9)

III. We Can't Fathom God
   A. A "fathom" is a 6 foot length of rope used to measure depth. Thus "to fathom" means to get to the bottom of something
   B. This is amply illustrated by:
       1. The study of the Word
       2. Computer technology. A novice knows more of computers than any man knows of God

IV. We Can't Outsmart God
   A. The basic idea of "outsmart" is that of being smarter than someone
   B. We are never smarter than God
       1. His knowledge is unlimited to the point of completeness
       2. Our knowledge is always limited

V. We Can't Escape God
   A. We are ultimately confronted

        1. The time lapse proves nothing
        2. Our confrontation is certain
   B. We will finally be accounted
        1. There will be an accounting
        2. We are filling the pages now, even though we may deny future accountability

VI. We Can't Resist God
   A. Men constantly try to resist God
   B. Resistance is another indication of His incomparability
        1. We resist only by His allowance
        2. We will be called into account for it

Conclusion:

The Prophet asks the following questions: To whom will you liken God? To what likeness will you compare Him? To whom shall God be equal? To whom can we compare God to make a likeness? The answer to all all those questions is nothing and no one. We can't understand Him, we can't fathom Him, we can't outsmart Him, we can't escape Him, and we can't resist Him. In what areas are you being unrealistic?

The Jealousy of God

Ezekiel 39:25

Introduction:

When God repeats something, you can be sure He really wants us to know it. Many themes are frequently repeated in Scripture. When that happens, we do well to take note. Let's look at a frequently repeated theme.

I. God Is a Jealous God

A. This is repeated in many passages:
1. Exodus 10:5; 34:14
2. Deuteronomy 4:24; 5:9; 6:15
3. Joshua 24:19
B. When something is repeated that often, we do well to try to find out what it is all about, what God is trying to tell us

II. God's Jealousy Is Different From Man's

A. Man's jealousy is a negative emotion and usually a very unattractive trait
1. It has to do with broken relationships
2. It expresses an excessive possessiveness
B. God's jealousy is different
1. It is to be very watchful in guarding or keeping something
2. It requires exclusive loyalty
C. God's jealousy centers on particular objects
1. He is jealous of the love of His people
2. He is jealous of other gods
3. He is especially jealous of His holy name (God is very fussy about His name and the things with which His name is linked)

III. God's Jealousy Is Important to Us

A. The basic issue:
1. God guards His name
2. We are named by that name (Christ is God). "Once you become a Christian, you are named by the name of Christ (God)"
3. Since God is protective about His name and we are named by it, we ought to be careful how we live
B. Specific details
1. We defile the name of the Lord when we use it in vain
2. We defile the name of the Lord when we sin

3. We defile the name of the Lord by a low-level general lifestyle
4. We defile the name of the Lord when we fail to speak of it, proclaim it, share it with other people
5. We defile the name of the Lord through lack of faith accomplishments
   a. We are designed to have unusual things happen in our lives
   b. God wants and waits to do the unusual for us
   c. When nothing unusual happens, it is a sign that there is something wrong with us
C. The particular applications
   1. Probably most of us never use His name in vain
   2. We are likely not involved in open sin
   3. We generally don't have low-level lifestyles
   4. We even speak to others at times
   5. But what of the unusual in our lives that really shows His power?

Conclusion:

God is jealous. We dare not tangle with Him. Where are you "messing" with His Holy name? What is there in your life to show that you "name His name"?